What Parents Need to about

Teen Risk Taking

Strategies for Reducing Problems Related to Alcohol, Other Drugs, Gambling and Internet Use

David A. Wolfe
Debbie Chiodo
Bruce Ballon
Gloria Chaim
Joanna L. Henderson

camh

| Health
mentale

SOUTHWARK LIBRARIES

SK 2640174 6

Library and Archives Canada Cataloguing in Publication

What parents need to know about teen risk taking : strategies for reducing problems related to alcohol, other drugs, gambling and Internet use / David A. Wolfe ... [et al.].

Issued also in French under title: Ce que les parents doivent savoir sur les comportements à risque des adolescents. Includes bibliographical references.

1. Risk-taking (Psychology) in adolescence--Prevention. 2. Peer pressure in adolescence.
3. Teenagers--Substance use--Prevention. 4. Parent and teenager. 5. Parenting. I. Wolfe, David A.
II. Centre for Addiction and Mental Health

RJ506.R57W43 2011   155.5'18   C2011-901945-0

ISBN: 978-0-88868-610-7 (PRINT)
ISBN: 978-0-88868-611-4 (PDF)
ISBN: 978-1-77052-284-8 (ePUB)
ISBN: 978-0-88868-612-1 (HTML)

Printed in Canada
Copyright © 2011 Centre for Addiction and Mental Health
No part of this work may be reproduced or transmitted in any form or by any means electronic or mechanical, including photocopying and recording, or by any information storage and retrieval system without written permission from the publisher—except for a brief quotation (not to exceed 200 words) in a review or professional work.

This publication may be available in other formats. For information about alternate formats or other CAMH publications, or to place an order, please contact Sales and Distribution:
Toll-free: 1 800 661-1111
Toronto: 416 595-6059
E-mail: publications@camh.net
Online store: http://store.camh.net

Website: www.camh.net

This book was produced by:
Development: Margaret Kittel Canale, CAMH
Editorial: Jacquelyn Waller-Vintar, CAMH; Sandra E. Martin
Design: Nancy Leung, CAMH
Print production: Christine Harris, CAMH

3517b / 08–2011 / PM066

© 2011 CAMH

Contents

© 2011 CAMH

© 2011 CAMH

What this book is about

You probably picked up this book because you want to know more about some of the risks your teenager faces today—and about some of the risky behaviours she may become involved in such as smoking, drinking and using other drugs, gambling or inappropriate use of the Internet. You likely want to know how to prevent or at least minimize your teen's experimentation with these risky behaviours. You want simple, practical advice and information on how to handle these situations and many more. Or you may simply feel you would benefit from advice about how to meet your teen's needs, "survive" the teenage years, and keep her safe and healthy all at the same time.

You may have noticed that some of the pressures on teens come in different forms today than in previous generations. Regardless of the form, pressure is pressure—and to teens the pressures can seem overwhelming at times. You, too, may feel overwhelmed by the issues your teen brings home.

Like it or not, teens will be faced with the pressure to experiment with tobacco, alcohol, other drugs and gambling, and they may find themselves in intimate situations for which they are not emotionally or physically ready. As a parent, you will be faced with difficult situations, balancing your teen's need to become more independent and autonomous while still providing the extra guidance and monitoring he needs at this time.

What works best in these parenting situations is a careful and practical approach—with a little bit of patience. You need to consider and understand your child's specific behaviour, the environment in which it occurred, the relationship dynamics involved and what the behaviour's purpose

© 2011 CAMH

serves. Seeking premature solutions or reacting without thinking things through can make a situation worse.

Before we can talk about prevention, you need to understand that adolescents are natural experimenters. In some instances, this tendency makes them the interesting and exciting individuals they are. But viewed in another way, this can be a scary period of time for adolescents as well as for their parents.

Knowing when your teen is ready to make decisions or try new "freedoms" without taking unnecessary risks is key. In essence, adolescence is about building trust and responsibility. Your teen wants you to trust that she is capable of making adult decisions and being responsible for them. You need to support your teen's need for trust and *autonomy* to a degree, while still remaining firm in your expectations of her.

As a parent, you have a powerful influence over your teen's risk-taking behaviour. Your teen looks to you for help and guidance in working out problems and in making decisions, including those related to smoking, drinking, using other drugs, gambling and becoming sexually active. Be a good listener, and give clear messages about the dangers associated with risky behaviours.

The purpose of this book—as with the other books in this series—is to give you a better understanding of the key issues pertaining to adolescent development—and how your role as a parent can make a difference in how your teen develops the ability to make good choices. This book will also provide you with information on how to better understand the new identity development taking place in your teen—and how the need to "fit in" or "be popular" can influence your teen to experiment with smoking, drinking, other drugs and gambling.

The challenge for parents, as you may have already discovered, is to support your teen's need to become more autonomous and independent, while helping to ensure he makes safe and healthy choices around the many risky decisions he faces during this period of development. Warning your teen about risks or consequences can only go so far—he needs to

© 2011 CAMH

know that you also understand the pressures he is sometimes under and that he can go to you for advice and support without fear of being scorned.

After reading this book you should have a better understanding of:

- what "experimenting" means during adolescence
- the types of pressures—real and imagined—your teen may experience and how these pressures influence her behaviour and decisions
- how to provide your teen with knowledge and guidance that he will respect
- ways to emphasize safety and responsibility while remaining relevant to your teen's life
- strategies for effective parenting that communicate positive messages and reduce conflict.

© 2011 CAMH

Why adolescence is so important

Shanta has a daughter who seems to make up her own life rules and has very few responsibilities around the house. Shanta is frustrated with the situation and doesn't know what to do. Shanta has lost track of her daughter's friends, doesn't want her going out at night or attending parties and is worried about her daughter's safety. "She won't listen to me. What can I do when she stomps out of the house and tells me I just don't understand what it's like to be a teenager in Canada? I stayed home with my parents and was more respectful."

Ramona always felt very close to her son and she can't understand what has happened. "Pablo started high school and suddenly I hardly know this person who lives with me. We used to talk about his day, his friends and his activities. Now I consider myself lucky if he gives me yes or no answers. I feel like he is shutting me out of his life and would rather spend all his time at his friend's house rather than at our own."

John adores his daughter Catherine. They have always had a fairly open relationship and he has never had reason not to trust her. But lately he is not sure what's going on. Catherine is missing her curfew, being irresponsible with the family car and insisting she be given more freedom. "I still trust her most of the time, but it's hard to know everything that's going on and when to be concerned."

© 2011 CAMH

If you are the parent of a teenager, these scenarios and evolving relation-ships will sound all too familiar to you and will be accompanied by a range of emotions—including concern, frustration, helplessness, anger, sense of failure, and fear related to your teen's behaviour and well-being. It seems like your previously co-operative child awoke one morning and suddenly became a character from a movie—someone you don't know so well anymore. You used to feel like the most important person in her life, and now you're another name on her speed dial. Your child used to love to spend time at home with you but that has all changed. You knew this could happen during the teen years, but do you ever really feel prepared with the understanding and confidence that everything will turn out okay?

We wrote this book because most parents of teens face these challenges and could use a little help. Remember, adolescence is a process of develop-ment: Change is usually good, and it's usually not easy or mistake-free. As a parent, it's better to be prepared than scared: Focus on the path ahead and help your teen be who he wants to be (after all, you know your child best).

Adolescence is so important because of the major developmental processes teens go through: They are becoming more independent—and they are learning to make their own decisions, resolve conflicts and manage stress. These decisions often have lifelong effects, and occur under tremendous (real and perceived) personal and social pressure.

BECOMING MORE INDEPENDENT

Adolescence is a time of changes and transformations for both the teenager and the parent. It is a time of negotiating new boundaries and rules, and a time of discovery and independence. With these changes, there are challenges you are all too familiar with: rebelliousness, defiance, disloyalty, conflicts, uncertainties and fear.

Yes, adolescence can be challenging—and it can also be rewarding, especially if you prepare for your role as the parent of a teen as much as

© 2011 CAMH

you prepared when you first became a parent! And (more good news!), despite these challenges, most adolescents emerge as healthy and responsible adults—and, delightfully, maintain positive and loving relationships with their parents throughout their own adulthood.

Simply put, your relationship with your teen changes! Obviously it has to change for your teen to learn to be independent—however, this simple fact often gets lost in your teen's day-to-day striving for autonomy. As your teen gradually requires greater independence and privacy, you must gradually respect that and, to some degree, grant it.

A crucial developmental process for adolescents is to develop a sense of who they are and who they want to become. This emerging "sense of self" will seem different at times from the "younger self" whom you came to know so well and (wait for it!) your teen might want to keep some of it private from you! Teens are trying to develop a sense of individuality, while attempting to "fit in" with what their peers, parents and other adults expect of them. When you stop and think about it, you'd probably agree that this process wasn't easy for you, and is probably even tougher in some ways for teens today. Given the pressures to be popular and accepted by peers (especially for girls) and to be seen as "cool" and strong (especially for boys), is it any wonder that they may "try on" new appearances, activities, and friendships, and test new boundaries and freedoms?

It is your task as the parent to help your teen progressively develop this new self, while ensuring he is safe, and making smart and healthy decisions. But it's not easy. Your teenager seems unpredictable. You are worried about the many influences he is exposed to daily. Your sense of control is diminishing—and this scares you.

What you need to know and understand is that even as teens gradually become more independent and rely on friends more than family, they still crave the comfort and the connection they have with their parents. They need to know that if something goes wrong, they have a safe place to come

© 2011 CAMH

home to and that you will be there when they need you. While teens want the approval of their friends like never before, they still need and want parents' love, respect and dependability.

You are and will remain a very important adult in your teen's life. Use that opportunity to help move your teen toward becoming a physically and emotionally healthy adult. Think of yourself as a guide: A guide offers direction, advice and wisdom at reasonable opportunities to promote a safe journey. A guide also offers warnings about potential dangers on the path ahead and makes sound decisions when things go wrong.

LEARNING TO MAKE DECISIONS

Teens must make decisions on a daily basis about so many aspects of their lives. Here are a few:

- What should I wear to school today? What's my style (for example, clothes, hair, makeup)?
- How do I cope with stress from school?
- How can I stand by my convictions?
- Who should I hang out with?
- What do I do if my friends are doing things I'm not comfortable with?
- What about smoking, drinking or using other drugs? Should I use them or not? Which ones are okay for me to try? How much should I use? Who do I use them with? Where do I use them?
- What should I do if I see rude comments and messages about my friends on Facebook or other social networking sites? What if the comments are about me?

It is sometimes difficult for teens to decide what choices they have in a particular situation.

© 2011 CAMH

Consider the following situation in which Yolanda is invited to her friend Leroy's house on Saturday night.

By agreeing to go to Leroy's house, these are just some of the situations Yolanda could need to make decisions about:

Whom to spend time with? Which crowds will be there?

What about her curfew? Is her curfew too early? Could she negotiate a later curfew? Or just wait and see?

What to tell her parents—who grew up in a different time, in a different culture and with different rules—or how much to tell them?

What if he offers her alcohol or other drugs? Should she say no? Maybe try something? And if so, what?

Is Leroy interested in being friends or in a relationship? If the latter, does he just want to "hook up"? Should she become sexually involved with Leroy?

Every activity and every decision has many layers, and all teens face them at one time or another. It is important for parents to talk to their teens about these types of issues whenever there is an opportunity— rather than just raising all these concerns when teens are going out.

© 2011 CAMH

LEARNING TO RELATE AS A YOUNG ADULT

One of the major changes you may have already noticed in your relationship with your teen is how uncommunicative he has become. Detailed conversations with you, once animated and exciting, have become shorter and more distant. Responses to your questions have become vague, even evasive.

The words "I don't know," "because" or "I'm fine" sometimes take on the bulk of your teen's discussions with you. You know she can speak more than just one-syllable words because you hear telephone conversations with friends that are animated and last for hours. More frustrating for you as a parent is the texting that can also go on for hours, but without the benefit of hearing even one side of the conversation. And yet, whatever it is you have to say, good or bad, it is always a chore for your teen to sit down and listen. In fact, if you could just get your teen to sit down with you some days, that would almost be good enough.

"Zits" used with the permission of the Zits Partnership, King Features Syndicate and the Cartoonsit Group. License 2010-307.

So why do teenagers do this? First of all, don't take it personally because it likely isn't about you. Some teenagers communicate less and seem distant because they think those are ways of gaining independence. They want to capture all of life's challenges on their own and make adult decisions on their own. And above all else, they don't want their parents telling them what to do or how to do it. By keeping conversations to a

© 2011 CAMH

minimum they avoid the risk of being questioned, challenged or denied a choice.

Secondly, it's their way of testing and fulfilling an important psychological need. They are trying to figure out whether something they have always known to be true and constant—your love and support—is going to change like everything else in their world. While it may be difficult to live with someone who is shutting you out of her life one minute and wanting you to be a part of it the next, trust that this will end.

By the time your teen is 17 or 18, more mature and emotionally independent, she will begin the next process of learning to relate to you as one adult to another. The key message to keep in mind throughout adolescence is love and connection. Teens may want to be on their own, but they still need you. You still matter to them and they still care about you.

One last point. It should come as no surprise that boys and girls differ significantly in terms of how they make decisions, resolve conflicts and manage stress during this active period of development. In Western culture, girls tend to prefer conversation and self-disclosure with peers—and they worry about what others think and say about them. Boys, on the other hand, prefer rough-and-tumble play, usually in larger groups, and encounter more overt verbal and physical conflict with peers.

These gender differences have important implications for development, because the trade-offs for girls and boys differ. The ways girls often learn to relate to others make them more vulnerable to emotional problems, such as anxiety and low self-esteem, and less vulnerable to behavioural problems. In contrast, the ways in which boys learn to relate to others increase their chances of developing behaviour problems, such as aggression and acting out, and protect them from developing emotional problems. (If you would like more information on this topic, we encourage you to read Rose & Rudolph, 2006.)

© 2011 CAMH

As parents, you need to be sensitive to your teen's style of relating to others, and to the pressures placed on him by the expectations of society, family, and cultural and spiritual beliefs and practices. You need to guide him as much as possible toward healthy relationships by being a role model for him and through providing him with opportunities to form relationships with a variety of peers and adults.

© 2011 CAMH

Why teens experiment and take risks (and why some don't)

There may be a perfect fit between being an adolescent, and the allure of substance use and other risk-taking behaviours.

Adolescents are impulsive and short-term thinkers. They are natural experimenters, and they want to fit in with their peers and peer culture. Teenagers think they can handle anything that comes their way, and many fail to understand or recognize the various consequences of their actions both in the short and long term. These developmental factors play a role in whether your teen "experiments" with substances, gambling or similar behaviours on occasion, or goes beyond experimentation to more dangerous use.

While things have changed (some for the better, others for the worse) since you were growing up, many of the pressures you faced as a teenager are the same ones your teen faces today. The need to fit in and to be liked transcends every generation. The desire for adult-like privileges, to wear the latest fashions, to attend the late-night parties, are what adolescents think is their "right"—something you may have felt as a teenager as well.

The attraction to experiment with alcohol and other drugs is no different than when you faced these choices and pressures. However, the potency of drugs available today, the easier accessibility to online information about "designer" or "cocktail" drugs, and the greater sophistication some teens have about ways to obtain alcohol and other drugs has increased. And the numerous ways in which society and the media market alcohol, gambling and sexual activity to teens sometimes seems overwhelming. These circumstances make it all the more important that

© 2011 CAMH

parents are informed about how their teens are influenced daily, and that they learn to communicate effectively to their teens about these topics.

Young people are bombarded by ads for alcohol and cigarettes in print, on TV, on the Internet and on the radio. Television commercials that portray young, attractive people at parties drinking beer or liquor expose underage teens to these images daily. While advertising is not the only reason teenagers experiment with alcohol, it is a major contributing factor. Youth who are exposed to alcohol advertising drink more, and more often, than those who are not. Research shows that underage drinking plays a significant role in risky sexual behaviour, including unwanted, unintended and unprotected sexual activity, as well as sex with different partners.

PRESSURES FACED BY TEENS

As a parent, you need to familiarize yourself with some of the pressures your teen may face. Teens are more likely to listen to what you have to say if you listen to them and have some understanding about (as well as have some respect for) what they have to say. You don't want them to make up stories or avoid you altogether so, to remain important in their lives, you need to recognize the pressures they often face—and remain focused on helping them develop trust and responsibility in managing such pressures.

We're not suggesting you give in, go along with or give up: We simply mean that parents need to make informed decisions and involve their teens, in the decisions as much as possible. We do suggest you avoid the alternatives of dictating the rules, threatening consequences and scaring (or boring) teens with lectures.

Naturally, teens want to fit in with their peers. If a friend offers them a drink or some marijuana at a party, they may go along with it because they want to be liked or feel part of the group. Peers' positive attitudes toward substance use, and the availability of alcohol and other drugs increase the likelihood of your son's or daughter's use.

© 2011 CAMH

Adolescents can feel intimidated and awkward in social situations, especially if they attend parties or gatherings with older teens. They may decide to drink alcohol or try other drugs to calm themselves down or feel "more relaxed." But whatever "reasons" teens use for trying substances, the impairment that can result from frequent or excessive use can be dangerous.

WHAT INCREASES TEEN RISK TAKING?

Trying to explain why an adolescent makes unsafe choices, such as binge drinking, is no easy task. Some familiar explanations made popular through TV shows and news reports oversimplify the causes as, for example, "he wanted his classmates to like him" or "her parents are divorced." However, the number of factors that potentially influence a teen's binge drinking and other unsafe actions defy simple explanations.

The steps teens take toward risk-taking behaviours usually go like this: First they experiment with new opportunities after taking an interest in the activity (such as smoking or gambling) through normal processes of awareness and curiosity. They may then decide to try out the activity based on their *attitudes* about the risks and benefits, their *beliefs* about what others may be doing, and the extent to which they feel they have control over the new activity (in other words, if they think they can do it safely).

Teens will hold positive attitudes about drinking, for example, if they weigh the risks and benefits and decide that the expected benefits outweigh the possible risks or costs. Their analysis is influenced by a number of factors, including the degree to which they think others (such as friends and family) drink, and their desire to please or comply with the wishes of important others (usually their peers). They may also feel pressure to drink if they overestimate how common the behaviour is among their peers and other people who are important to them. Interestingly, studies show that most teens greatly overestimate how many of

© 2011 CAMH

their friends are having sex, drinking alcohol and smoking marijuana (see Wolfe, Jaffe & Crooks, 2006).

Because risk-taking and health-compromising behaviours occur in the adolescent's social world, their relationships with family members and peers play a crucial role in shaping their attitudes and desires. When they spend time with others who like to drink or smoke, or are exposed to many positive images of these activities in movies and other forms of entertainment, they have the opportunity to observe and imitate these behaviours ("how do you do it?"); receive encouragement and support ("it's fun—try it!"; "you're one of us"); and expect positive social ("you're cool") and physiological consequences ("it makes you feel good") from participation. Through these influences, teens quickly learn to expect more personal benefits than costs when they smoke, drink or gamble, increasing their desire to take more risks and try other new things.

Remember that teens' decisions are shaped by their relationships with important role models (past and present) who influence their current beliefs, intentions and feelings of effectiveness in given situations. As a parent, you are one of these important role models.

Remember, too, that adolescents' brains have not fully matured, especially in terms of "social judgment" and the ability to make balanced decisions (see a fuller discussion of this in the first book in the series, *What Parents Need to Know about Teens: Facts, Myths and Strategies*). Teens' curiosity and interest are piqued by their exposure to new activities and opportunities, but they lack the judgment and knowledge needed to delay gratification and make safer choices. This is why the adults in their lives— and not their peer group—play such an important role in helping them make safe and responsible decisions.

© 2011 CAMH

WHAT REDUCES TEEN RISK TAKING?

We have considerable evidence about the factors that protect teens from making poor choices or getting into dangerous situations. The three most powerful factors are described below.

Parental monitoring

Be involved in your teen's life in a positive and supportive manner, and don't be afraid to "assist" them in coming to the best decision.

Quality of the parent-teen relationship

You've spent many years being a positive and available parent to your child—and that pays off during adolescence. Trust, communication and support from a parent go a long way in providing teens with the skills and confidence they need to resist pressures. Even if there have been problems between you in the past, it's never too late to restore these valuable qualities in your relationship.

Parent-teen communication about risks and responsibilities

Share your thoughts and knowledge about risky behaviours such as using drugs, engaging in sexual activity and aggressive behaviour (including, for example, in-person or cyberbullying). Speak in an informative, non-judgmental fashion (don't lecture!). Be clear about the behaviours you expect from your teen so she knows what you want her to do—and not just want you want her not to do.

We develop these risk-reduction strategies further in the last two chapters.

© 2011 CAMH

When does experimenting become a problem?

How does a parent achieve a balance between a child's need to grow and take risks, and his need to stay safe?

In the following sections, we discuss what are normal or typical behaviours (yet perhaps still worrisome to parents) as children move into adolescence. We highlighht some early warning signs of potential problem behaviours, followed by more serious indicators that a problem exists.

WHAT ARE TYPICAL TEEN BEHAVIOURS?

Substance use and other risk behaviours fall along a continuum of behaviours extending from no involvement, to natural curiosity, to experimentation, to periodic or social use, to regular (even daily) involvement.

Most teens fall somewhere in the middle of this continuum. In the case of substance use, for example, most adolescents experiment with substances on occasion without experiencing adverse effects and without moving on to heavier, problematic use. However, there are always some risks associated with any amount of substance use—including risks (and increased risks with increased use) of injury or death because of health problems directly linked to the substance use, drinking (or using other drugs) and driving, sexual assault and aggression. Frequent and prolonged use of alcohol and other drugs may also interfere with the development of important psychosocial skills and educational achievement.

And you've likely heard stories about (or can easily picture) the following troubling scenarios: Teenagers cyberbullying on Facebook; adolescents

© 2011 CAMH

posting semi-nude pictures of themselves on YouTube; 12-year-old girls making "friends" in chat rooms and on MySpace; young adults battling demons through the night with other cybergamers in the World of Warcraft; university students glued to online casino sites gambling the last of their student loan money; a well-rounded, high-achieving teen taking ecstasy for the first time at a concert and being found dead the following morning. These situations do, of course, happen but they are not the norm.

Here are some findings from a 2009 survey of Ontario students (Paglia-Boak et al., 2009) in grades 7 to 12, based on what students said about their involvement in these activities during the 12 months before the survey. This annual survey goes to randomly selected, publicly funded public, Catholic and alternative schools in Ontario.

You may be surprised to discover that, in 2009, almost one-third (31 per cent) of students reported using no substances during the past year. You may be further surprised by the drugs used most by students: alcohol (58 per cent of students), cannabis (26 per cent), non-medical use (i.e., not prescribed for them by a doctor) of prescription drugs (20 per cent) and tobacco (12 per cent). In addition, fewer students are using alcohol, tobacco and cannabis by Grade 6 (a decline from 1981 to 2009); and the use of most drugs decreased from 1999 to 2009. Following are more statistics about these and other drugs, about drug-related behaviours and about gambling and gaming.

Alcohol

In the survey, alcohol use includes drinking beer, wine or liquor. The statistics also include those students who drank only on special occasions.

- Alcohol is the most commonly used drug by Ontario students in grades 7 to 12 (58 per cent). This also means that 42 per cent did not drink any alcohol.

© 2011 CAMH

- Fewer students are drinking alcohol today (58 per cent) compared to students in 1999 (66 per cent). Among those students who do drink, 10 per cent report drinking at least once a week.

- Not surprisingly, the number of students drinking alcohol increases with grade, ranging from 23 per cent in Grade 7 to 83 per cent in Grade 12.

- About one-quarter of students report heavy drinking (binge drinking or becoming drunk) at least once during the four weeks before completing the survey. Binge drinking (drinking five or more drinks on one occasion) increases by grade, ranging from three (3) per cent of Grade 7 students to 49 per cent of Grade 12 students. Similarly, four (4) per cent of Grade 7 students reported being drunk compared to 43 per cent of those in Grade 12.

- One in eight (12 per cent) licensed drivers in grades 10 to 12 drove within an hour of consuming two or more drinks. Male drivers (15 per cent) are more likely than female drivers (8 per cent) to drink and drive.

- About one-quarter (23 percent) of students have been a passenger in a vehicle driven by someone who had been drinking alcohol.

Cannabis

In the survey, cannabis includes marijuana, hashish and hash oil.

- Cannabis is the second most commonly used drug by Ontario students in grades 7 to 12 (26 per cent).

- The number of students using cannabis increases with grade, ranging from one (1) per cent in Grade 7 to 46 per cent in Grade 12.

- About one in six (17 per cent) licensed drivers in grades 10 to 12

© 2011 CAMH

drove within one hour of using cannabis. Male drivers (21 per cent) are more likely than female drivers (11 per cent) to drive after using cannabis.

Non-medical use of prescription drugs

The non-medical use of prescription drugs (that is, use without a doctor's prescription) by adolescents is increasing in North America. The following numbers indicate the percentage of students in grades 7 to 12 using these substances without a prescription.

- The non-medical use of prescription opioid pain relievers (such as Percocet, Percodan, Tylenol #3, Demerol, OxyContin or codeine) is the third most commonly used drug category by Ontario students in grades 7 to 12 (18 per cent). About three-quarters (74 per cent) reported getting the pain relief pills from home.

- Two (2) per cent of students used stimulant drugs (such as Ritalin, Concerta and Adderall) that are normally used to treat attention deficit / hyperactivity disorder (ADHD) in children. The students used these drugs for non-medical purposes such as suppressing their appetites, staying awake, increasing their ability to focus and to experience euphoria.

- Five (5) per cent of students took other stimulants (also known as amphetamines), such as diet pills or stay-awake pills.

Tobacco

In the survey, tobacco use refers to smoking cigarettes.

- Tobacco is the fourth most commonly used drug by Ontario students in grades 7 to 12 (12 per cent). More than half (58 per cent) of those who smoked said they got their cigarettes from a friend or family member.

© 2011 CAMH

- The number of students who smoke increases with grade, ranging from one (1) per cent in Grade 7 to 20 per cent in Grade 12.

- About one-fifth (18 per cent) of smokers may be dependent on cigarettes.

Other illegal drugs

The use of other illegal drugs (that is, not including cannabis) is generally much lower than the use of alcohol, tobacco, cannabis or the non-medical use of prescription drugs.

- Two (2) per cent of students used LSD, one (1) per cent used PCP and five (5) per cent used other hallucinogens (such as mescaline and psilocybin).

- One (1) per cent of students used methamphetamine (also known as speed). One (1) per cent used crystal methamphetamine (also known as ice), a smokable form of methamphetamine. Three (3) per cent used methylenedioxymethamphetamine (known as ecstasy or MDMA).

- Three (3) per cent of students used cocaine; one (1) per cent used crack cocaine.

- One (1) percent of students used heroin.

Gambling

- In the survey (Paglia-Boak et al., 2010), gambling included the following activities: playing cards, bingo or dice for money; betting money in sports pools, at a casino in Ontario or over the Internet; betting money on video gambling machines, slot machines or other gambling machines; and buying lottery tickets.

© 2011 CAMH

- Male students are more likely than female students to engage in most gambling activities.
- The percentage of students reporting gambling problems has decreased over the past 10 years to three (3) per cent.

Video gaming

In the survey, students were asked about video game playing on a computer, on TV or in an arcade.

- Males (32 per cent) are more likely than females (six [6] per cent) to play video games daily.
- Sixteen (16) per cent of males have a video gaming problem compared to four (4) per cent of females.

The above statistics point out that most youth do not develop problems with substance use, gambling or video gaming—in fact, most youth are well-adjusted, get along with their parents, do their homework and have good friends. The statistics further suggest that youth use substances today much as they did in previous generations—and most do so in a way that does not adversely affect their lives.

Even though many teens engage in behaviours that involve risk taking, most do not develop problems with these behaviours—but some do. The question you likely want answered is: How do I know if my teen is developing a problem? What are the signs I need to watch for?

Before answering that question, we want to describe in more detail what the various levels of "use" or "activity" might look like.

© 2011 CAMH

CONTINUUM OF RISK—FROM NO PROBLEM TO A SERIOUS PROBLEM

We spoke earlier in the chapter about a continuum of behaviours ranging from no involvement in risk behaviours to regular, even daily, involvement. Following are signs to look for in your teen regarding her "level of use" of the risk behaviours we've been discussing.

Experimental or occasional use

This level of use or activity has no significant or detrimental impact on a person's life. For example, your teen might drink wine with family or at religious ceremonies. He may use the Internet for short periods daily to chat with friends or find information.

Problematic use

Activities or use occasionally cause problems. For example, your teen may stay up late one night playing games on the Internet—and the next day she misses a class or fails an exam. Hopefully the lesson learned will make her more careful, and her life will continue without any major negative consequences.

Abuse or harmful involvement

A pattern begins to develop where your teen's life is ruled by the need to engage in his chosen activities (e.g., substance use, gambling, the Internet, gaming, sex or other risk behaviours). The frequency (e.g., daily use) or severity (e.g., binge drinking) of his behaviours have a harmful impact on one or more areas of his life (e.g., social, academic, vocational, mental, physical or spiritual). For example, your teen's daily late-night gambling activities result in failing grades and dropping out of school. His missed social engagements and stealing from people he knows to finance his gambling activities strains his relationships with family and friends.

    In the case of alcohol and other drugs, the body becomes so used

© 2011 CAMH

to the drug that it needs more and more of it to achieve the same effects. With gambling, gaming and Internet use, a person can become dependent on the feeling he gets while engaging in these activities—a feeling created by the release of pleasure chemicals already in the brain. These brain chemicals can affect a person differently, depending on the setting. For example, someone may experience more pleasure doing the activity with friends than by himself.

Some teens may begin to feel a sense of mastery at these activities— often because they don't feel masterful in other areas of their lives (perhaps due to social anxiety, being bullied, physical ailments or trauma issues). For example, engaging in gambling or gaming activities and anticipating a win can be very exciting—and an actual win can create a feeling of euphoria. This can make youth feel important, successful, skilled—and happy. However, a loss can replace happy or euphoric feelings with anxiety, sadness, desperation, frustration and anger.

Both sets of emotional paths or extremes—euphoria and anger—can make people feel drawn to repeat the activity. This form of reinforcement is one of the strongest psychological aspects of becoming "hooked" on these activities.

WHAT ARE THE EARLY WARNING SIGNS?

A yellow flag: Age at first use

On a positive note, the percentage of youth starting to use substances at an early age has significantly declined over the years for alcohol, tobacco and cannabis—a fact that should not be overlooked. Efforts at education and prevention over the past two decades may be paying off in terms of reducing some youth risk behaviours.

Typically, substance use peaks around late adolescence and begins to decline during young adulthood, as young people take up adult roles of work, marriage and parenthood. For some teens, however, a pattern

© 2011 CAMH

of early-onset risk taking may signal a more troublesome course that can threaten their well-being in both the short and long term.

Although a certain amount of substance use during adolescence is normal behaviour, some things increase or decrease the risk of long-term problems or injuries. The age at which a teen first uses alcohol, tobacco or other drugs is one of the best predictors of long-term problems. The Canadian National Longitudinal Survey of Youth (NLSY) found, for example, that the odds of developing alcohol dependence decreased by nine per cent for each year that the onset of drinking was delayed. In general, alcohol use before age 14 is a strong predictor of subsequent problems with alcohol use, especially when early drinking is followed by a rapid increase in the amount of alcohol consumed.

Your concern is particularly warranted when high-risk behaviors begin well before adolescence, are ongoing rather than occasional, and occur among a group of people your teen spends time with. Indeed, most risk and problem behaviors co-occur, so an indication of one problem is often a signal that others may be happening or on their way.

A red flag: Problems in relationships and with dependability

Although experimentation with substances is commonplace among teenagers, it is not harmless: Substance use lowers inhibitions, reduces judgment, and increases the risk of physical harm and sexual assault. For example, a survey of Canadian high school students found that alcohol use influenced the practice of, or involvement in, many other high-risk behaviours, most notably unsafe sexual activity, smoking, and drinking and driving (Feldman et al., 1999).

Teens who use alcohol and other drugs are more likely to have sexual intercourse at an earlier age, have more sexual partners and have greater risk of getting sexually transmitted diseases. Substance use is also a risk factor for unhealthy weight control (such as taking diet pills or laxatives), suicidal thoughts, and mood and anxiety disorders (Swahn et al., 2008). Moreover, alcohol use is associated with dating violence: Girls who report

© 2011 CAMH

being in a relationship involving dating violence (either as the person being assaulted or the person doing the assaulting) are five times more likely to use alcohol than girls in non-violent relationships; boys in such relationships are 2.5 times more likely to use alcohol (Pepler et al., 2002).

It is important to model the values and standards you expect of your teen to ensure he can deal with the world of sex and substances he is likely to face. Every teen will have to choose whether to drink, use other drugs or have sex. As a parent, you have more influence over how your teen responds to these situations than does anyone else.

Following are examples of "red flag" signs you'll want to pay close attention to, because they may indicate your teen has a problem with one of more of the risky behaviours we focus on in this book:

- engaging in certain dating and sexual behaviours (such as having sex with different partners or not using condoms for protection, although rarely will your teen disclose this information to you). Teens who participate in these types of behaviours may be more likely to have a substance use problem or engage in other activities that may pose health risks. Of course, having conversations with your child about these topics may be stressful—and you might not get straight answers. Present your comments as education and concern for your teen's well-being

- money and objects disappearing from the house

- developing new groups of friends whom you never get to see (this might also include his social network on the computer)

- school work starting to be affected in a negative way

- a steady downward shift in your teen's ability to function in any aspect of life. At the same time, though, most adolescents are going through lots of changes and trying out different identities. So a downward shift in functioning is a concern only if it keeps going down

- engaging in substance use, gambling and gaming in a way that affects his school work, his job or his relationships

© 2011 CAMH

- getting in trouble with the law
- engaging in dangerous activities like driving drunk or stoned (i.e., high on cannabis or other drugs)
- if substance use, gambling or gaming is a central part of his life and is occurring almost daily.

Any one of these activities may indicate that your teen has a serious problem and needs help.

MORE TROUBLESOME SIGNS

When one or more of the following behaviours occur—and appear to be associated with the use or overuse of an activity—this should trigger concern in the family (we say "appear" because there are always other possible explanations for problems, and we suggest you gather information and speak to other knowledgeable people before drawing conclusions. Notably, co-occurring issues like depression or anxiety can also explain the changes below and should be ruled out before assuming a problem is related to substance use, gambling, Internet use or gaming):

- sleep disturbances—this includes sleeping too much or very little; sleeping at school because he doesn't sleep at night; sleeping all day without your realizing that he stays up all night playing on a computer; or using cannabis to treat insomnia
- appetite disturbances—this includes being so absorbed with a video game that she skips meals; getting the "munchies" (i.e., increased appetite), induced by cannabis use; losing weight because the amphetamines she's taking suppress her appetite; feeling anxious after losing money gambling; and feeling nauseous
- withdrawal from his usual social activities—this could result from hanging out with peers that you never get to see, spending more time on the computer and hiding the sites and activities he connects with,

© 2011 CAMH

and staying home because of a lack of sleep and reduced energy

- spending less time with family and friends (although she may claim that many of her relationships are now online)

- worsening hygiene—this may occur if your teen chooses engaging in the problem behaviour over spending time looking after her personal care needs, possibly resulting in bad breath, body odour, uncombed hair and wearing the same clothes every day

- mood changes—this includes radical mood shifts (from the effects of substance use) to the degree that your teen's behaviour is almost unpredictable; or exhibiting extreme anger and irritability when someone interrupts the activity she's involved with (such as being in an online role-playing game)

- personality changes—these include being secretive, aloof, irritable and seemingly a different person than before

- lying, stealing and other similar activities—examples include money missing from your wallet, the disappearance of the DVD player that was in the basement and finding out your teen is not at a friend's house as she said she was

- dropping school marks

- difficulties maintaining jobs—problematic signs include showing up late for work, being unmotivated, being unkempt and having poor concentration

- not doing chores

- damaging her social reputation—this includes her friends calling her slang names that indicate they think of her as someone who has a substance use problem, is sexually promiscuous, is a thief, has a mental health problem or is a "loser."

© 2011 CAMH

A closer look at Internet use, gambling and gaming

Many parent groups and health care providers want to have gaming and Internet "addiction" recognized as a unique condition. It's important to recognize, however, that there can be many reasons why people develop difficulties with these media—just as there are many reasons why they may develop problems with substance use.

In many instances, teens' problem behaviours around Internet use and gaming arise out of a failure to find a healthy coping strategy for underlying mental health and stress-related problems they have, including:

- Asperger's syndrome—may drive them to learn everything about a topic by constantly researching it
- obsessive gambling—may keep them stuck on casino sites
- social anxiety—may keep them in chat rooms and role-play gaming worlds where they don't have to meet people face to face
- posttraumatic stress—may lead them to chat rooms where they seek others with whom they can re-enact traumatic situations they've experienced
- obsessive compulsive disorder—may keep them tied to the Internet, obsessed with a topic or game
- substance use problems—may lead them to order prescription medication and other drugs via e-mail, or to research ways to use drugs
- sexual "addiction"—may drive them to seek and download pornography
- self-harm—may lead them to chat rooms where youth share their thoughts and techniques about suicide and other self-harm behaviours, such as cutting and burning themselves
- any number of other difficult life events, such as loneliness, being bullied or parental divorce.

As you can see, the technology is not the sole issue—it's really how the chosen activity interacts with a person's unique makeup that determines

© 2011 CAMH

whether the seeds of a problem exist. For example, not all people who use a drug become dependent on the substance—and neither do all teens who play a particular video game become hooked on it to the point that it inter-feres with their lives. Understanding the problem includes understanding the features of the game, the mental and physical health of your teen, and the environment (e.g., family and peer relationships, economic status) in which your teen lives.

Remember, one of the most visible ways of knowing whether your teen has a problem with something is if she starts to function less well in one or more areas of her life (such as school, sports, leisure time or self-care).

People often consider Internet use or video game playing as a problem or an "addiction" based on the amount of time someone spends online and/or playing games. Instead, what counts is what a person spends his time doing and what that outlay of time does to the person. Consider the following examples.

> **Teen A** spends three hours a day playing online chess. He gets good grades at school, maintains his friendships, eats and sleeps well, and functions well in all other aspects of his life.

> **Teen B** spends seven hours a day (mostly at night) engaging in online role-playing games. She has disrupted her sleep cycle, beginning a chain of consequences that include arriving late to school and having falling grades. (As parents, you'll want to ask yourselves how this situation developed. Has it been going on for a long time, or did it develop suddenly? Who is paying for the games? If you are aware of the situation, why have you allowed it to go on this way?)

> **Teen C** spends 20 minutes a week playing online poker. He regularly uses one of his parents' credit cards (without permission) to pay for his gambling. He usually breaks even, but recently he lost more

© 2011 CAMH

than $8,000 in 10 minutes. (Parents checking credit card state-ments would catch this activity eventually. Unfortunately, many Internet sites have special "starter" gambling options where beginners play with "play" money. If they accumulate enough play money, they can convert it to real money—and they can do this under the age of 18. Can you see how this could lure a youth or any vulnerable person?)

A closer look at substance use

Substance use usually occurs as a result of social influence. For example, studies show that peer pressure and media influence can contribute to the development of mild substance use problems in youth; and that youth who develop more severe problems do so as a result of biological, psychological and familial factors—such as self-medicating with alcohol or other drugs to cope with or relieve unwanted emotional states.

Substance use problems (including dependence on one or more drugs) differ in youth compared to adults in several ways.

- Youth often experience more tolerance and fewer withdrawal symptoms and medical problems.

- The early onset of substance use, and intense and frequent use, may indicate a teen has a substance use problem.

- The quicker a youth increases the amount he uses of a substance and how often he uses it, the greater the risk that he will develop a substance use problem.

- Youth usually use more than one substance at a time—a practice that is less common in adults.

As with gambling and other risk behaviours, a youth's substance use may or may not develop into problems. The most important factors that determine whether a teen will develop problems include the substance she uses, the way in which she uses it and how all of this interacts with her individual characteristics.

© 2011 CAMH

DEPENDENCE

- using a large amount of a drug over a long period of time
- the inability to cut down or control one's use of the drug
- spending a great deal of time in drug-use related activities, such as seeking out the drug
- a reduction in important school, social and recreational activities due to one's drug use
- continued drug use even though the person experiences serious physical or psychological problems as a result of the drug use.

TOLERANCE

- the body's adaptation to repeated exposure to a drug
- a particular dose of the drug producing a less intense effect in the body
- the need to increase the dose of the drug to achieve the same effect as when the first dose was taken.

WITHDRAWAL

- a set of physical symptoms (sometimes dramatic) that occur when someone who is dependent on a drug suddenly stops using the drug
- experiencing the opposite effects of what the person experienced using the drug.

© 2011 CAMH

Consider the following scenario: We have five cannabis "joints" that contain the same amount of THC and additives that are commonly found in cannabis. We give a joint to five youth of the same age. The following descriptions show how each youth may have a different reaction even though each is smoking the same thing. After, we'll explain why this may occur.

Teen A *feels nothing. He does not even experience a "buzz" (happy sensation).*

Teen B *experiences a "buzz" and feels relaxed. A while later, she feels hungry.*

Teen C *experiences a "big buzz" and feels relaxed. Then he gets "the spins" (a feeling of vertigo) and vomits.*

Teen D *experiences a slight feeling of paranoia for several hours— her anxiety increases, her heart rate speeds up, and she senses that she is being watched.*

Teen E *develops a mild delusion (i.e., a fixed, false belief) that someone plans to harm him. This belief frightens him so much that he locks the doors and gets a knife. After a few hours, the delusion disappears.*

All of the above outcomes are possible for teens who use cannabis. While these are the typical outcomes, some youth may experience more extreme reactions (e.g., suicidal thoughts, psychosis) from using cannabis. The range of outcomes highlights the need to understand what a substance can do and raises the question: "What makes some youth more vulnerable to developing problems with certain drugs?"

© 2011 CAMH

Here are some factors that may raise the risk of developing substance use problems for youth:

- a mental health problem—some mental health problems, such as attention-deficit / hyperactivity disorder, depression, anxiety, conduct problems and learning difficulties, emerge in childhood and later increase the risk that a young person will develop substance use problems. Other mental health problems, such as bipolar disorder and schizophrenia, tend to first appear in adolescence and young adulthood, as do substance use behaviours

- certain temperamental and biological factors—examples include thrill seeking; problems controlling emotions; and the reduced ability to plan, pay attention, reason, exercise good judgment, control body movements or avoid behaving aggressively

- low resilience (the ability to "bounce back" from difficulties or challenges)

- low self-esteem

- difficulty controlling the intensity of feelings—this is often linked to difficulties with self-soothing and coping

- poor social skills

- a history of sexual or physical abuse

- living in a family with certain characteristics—examples include having a parent with an antisocial personality disorder; genetic or adoptive parents with substance use problems; absentee or unavailable parents; a mother with depression; families with permissive attitudes toward drug use; and a mother's heavy prenatal alcohol use (resulting in fetal alcohol effects in the child)

- associating with friends with conduct problems, substance use behaviours or both

© 2011 CAMH

- lacking positive role models, or admiring poor role models
- exposure to certain social variables—examples include living in a low-income family; lacking safety in the community or neighbourhood (e.g., because of gang activity)
- using so-called "gateway" drugs (such as tobacco, alcohol and cannabis) that may lead to the use of other drugs.

Risk-taking behaviours that interfere with a youth's social, academic, vocational, psychological, physical or interpersonal spheres are of major concern. Once such a pattern becomes established, it may indicate the presence of a health problem (for example, depression, diabetes, disability) or negative circumstances (for example, trauma, family conflict) that indicate you will need to seek professional help for your teen as soon as possible. We discuss some of the steps parents can take and list additional resources later in the book.

© 2011 CAMH

Strategies for effective parenting: What your teen needs from you

While caring for young children can be challenging, you understand that it is your job as parents to meet all their needs. You respond to their physical needs by providing them with food, clothing, shelter—and bandages for their cuts and scrapes. You address their emotional, psychological and spiritual needs with love and guidance. As your children grow, you know you have a responsibility to teach them how to make the best decisions. Some of those decisions seemed overwhelmingly complicated at the time yet, with the decisions facing today's teens, they seem simple in retrospect.

Consider, for example, the following questions—and how you might respond to an eight-year-old compared to a teenager.

Can I hang out with Sally after school?

Can I sleep over at Vikram's house?

Can I stay for another hour?

Can I have $2 to buy an ice cream from the ice cream truck?

I feel sick. Can I stay home from school today?

© 2011 CAMH

While the implications of each behaviour and your responses to them were likely straightforward when your child was eight, these questions take on a whole new meaning when coming from your teenager. The questions may now signal all kinds of risks and dangers for your child—particularly related to the availability of tobacco, alcohol and other drugs, and access to gambling, gaming and the Internet. Here are some of the things you'll likely want to know from your teen.

Where are you and Sally going after school? Who else will be there? What crowd does Sally hang out with?

Are Vikram's parents in town? I know they travel a lot and leave Vikram home alone. Is Vikram the one who is into some weird character in some computer game?

I heard your cell phone ring in the middle of the night. It disturbed everyone's sleep. Could you please turn it off when you go to bed?

What happened to the $40 I gave you two days ago when you needed to buy bus tickets? You must have quite a bit of money left over.

Why do you feel sick? Was there a lot of drinking last night at Katrine's party?

These types of situations can get increasingly complicated, specially as teens push back, telling you that they want to make their own decisions—telling you either directly by saying things like "don't tell me what to do!" or indirectly by ignoring you and doing the opposite of what you tell them to do.

© 2011 CAMH

So what does your teen need from you to effectively navigate the teen years and deal with the pressures to fit in, to perform and to meet the various expectations of peers and teachers as well as parents? How can teens experiment and take the risks they need to take to figure out who they are and who they want to become?

In the first book in the series, we introduced a number of general strategies for parenting teens. We revisit the strategies here (and add a few more)—with an emphasis on how the strategies apply to teen risk-taking behaviours.

KEEP UP YOUR PARENTING ROLE

Continue to be the wonderful parent you've always been. Be there for your teen as you were when she was younger. And remember that your role and hers have changed and will continue to change as she moves from childhood to adulthood.

In the first book, we listed some essential things teens generally need from parents. We're repeating the information here, because it has relevance to teens' smoking, drinking, other drug use and gambling. Your teen needs:

- information about the choices, responsibilities and consequences that go along with the new opportunities and pressures your teen will face

- to be prepared, not scared, to handle the pressures of adolescence

- to feel that your teen can rely on you for understanding, support, information and guidance (even if it means setting firm limits)

- you to model positive ways to handle conflicts, disappointments, risks and pressures from others, including you

- to feel connected not only to friends but also to school, family and community

- to feel appreciated

© 2011 CAMH

- to be seen as a person (rather than as a potential problem)
- to be treated fairly
- guidance in problem solving and decision making so your teen can think for herself and be involved in the solutions.

There is an abundance of information about tobacco, alcohol, other drugs and gambling coming at teens every day. They hear about it at school, on the radio, on TV, on the Internet, through their friends—the list is endless. The information is more or less accurate and useful, depending on the source and on your child, and how she interprets and uses the information. Of course, the information your teen receives is often within the context of relationships, sex and aggressive behaviour.

Your relationship with your child is one of the most important mediators of this information. This does not mean that you must be an expert on these topics, but it is useful for you to know where you and your teen can find reliable sources. Some teens will be more adept at accessing this type of information than you are—and you might want to access the information together. The key is to ensure that your teen understands your values and expectations, and that he believes that you trust and respect him.

SEE YOUR TEEN AS AN INDIVIDUAL

We've noted throughout this book that teens, parents and others hold stereotypes about adolescence. A common stereotype is the image of the rebellious, wild teen who constantly butts heads with mom and dad. While this may be the case for some teens—and this is an emotional time for both teens and their parents—that stereotype certainly does not represent most teens.

The danger of unfavourable stereotypes is that they can have significant negative effects on the well-being of young people. Teens can be

© 2011 CAMH

impressionable: When they hear stereotypes repeated by you or others, they may begin to believe the stereotypes are true and act accordingly. Take, for example, the situation of a young person who is working hard in math but getting poor marks. If he is told that he is stupid or lazy, "just like all teens," he may believe the comments and just give up. If he is told, however, that everyone learns differently and is offered some assistance to explore options, he may feel optimistic and engage in a process that helps him improve his math skills. Similarly, a young person who constantly hears (from people, including his parents) that all teens take drugs, will likely take drugs to meet those expectations.

In addition, the changes you see in your teen are not simply a result of his mood, hormones or even a "phase." By referring to his behaviour, his change of attitude, or his new style of dress as a phase or a mood swing, you send the message that you accept the stereotypes and are not prepared to see him as the unique human being he is and wants to be.

SHOW THAT YOU ARE INTERESTED

Treat your teen with respect and maturity, and maintain your firm expectations of her and her behaviour. Maintain positive communication—or any communication that is constructive and respectful.

You may be wondering about how to connect and communicate with your teen when it seems like she wants nothing to do with you. The key with uncommunicative teens is that while they may not want to talk to you, there is no reason why you cannot talk to them. Be interested in your teen's activities and friends. Ask questions about school, homework and her teachers. Talk about things that matter to her: music, dating, clothes or sports. Ask questions you may not want to hear the answers to. And really listen to what she has to say.

© 2011 CAMH

"Zits" used with the permission of the Zits Partnership, King Features Syndicate and the Cartoonsit Group. License 2010-307.

UNDERSTAND HOW YOUR TEEN'S DEVELOPMENT AFFECTS YOUR RELATIONSHIP

Consider the following scenario with Teresa and her teens, Maria, 18 and Eduardo, 15. (We will come back to these characters throughout the rest of this chapter as we apply relevant parenting strategies.)

Teresa is a single parent who often doesn't get home from work until 7 or 8 o'clock in the evening. By the time she gets home she is exhausted and is relieved if her children Maria, 18, and Eduardo, 15, have eaten dinner and are settled in their rooms or the basement (usually separately), hopefully getting some homework done.

Maria and Eduardo are supposed to come home after school unless they have programs or specific plans. Teresa does not permit them to have friends over when she is not home.

One day, Teresa isn't feeling well and leaves work early. She gets home around 4:30 p.m. and notices a pungent smell (burning?) coming from the basement. She is concerned that there is a fire

© 2011 CAMH

and starts calling the children's names. No one responds. She goes down to the basement and feels her senses overwhelmed by the smoke in the air (the smell now identifiable as marijuana), the blaring music, and a mess of empty junk food wrappers and pop cans.

Eduardo is staring intently at the computer and doesn't look up. Teresa hears the toilet flush and the sound of footsteps running up the stairs, followed by the front door slamming.

Teresa feels like screaming and yelling. She wants to scold Eduardo for breaking "all the rules" and she wants to conclude by grounding him "for life."

For Teresa to respond effectively to this situation, she will need to take some time to consider what has happened: Has Eduardo behaved like this before? Is this new behaviour for him? If it is new behaviour, what is going on to make him behave differently?

Teresa will also want to consider the following questions: Who was in the house with Eduardo? Was this someone new, or one of the friends he usually hangs out with? Does Eduardo usually break the rules and take risks? How does Eduardo feel about what happened? Did Eduardo smoke marijuana? Did he feel coerced into using marijuana? Does he need help with managing pressure from peers to do things he is uncomfortable with?

Build on your good relationship

As Teresa ponders these and other questions, the key factor she needs to keep in mind is the importance and the power of her relationship with Eduardo.

© 2011 CAMH

Much as Teresa's senses were overwhelmed by the "changes" she experienced when she descended into the basement, Eduardo has likely been overwhelmed by all the changes and new experiences he is undergoing as an adolescent and newcomer to Canada. He is coping with physical, emotional and brain changes. He is striving to assert his independence, partly by experimenting with new roles and behaviours. He is inundated with new experiences, such as watching movies that have increasingly explicit scenes of violence and sexuality, going to concerts unsupervised where alcohol and marijuana use are everywhere, travelling on school trips where supervision is limited, figuring out who he fits in with, and learning to navigate the Internet, and ever-evolving social networks and media. It is a challenge for him to integrate and make sense of all of this new information—and always make good decisions. And, lastly, impulsivity is part of adolescent "wiring" and should be expected.

Typical parent's question: What were you thinking?

Honest teen's response: I wasn't thinking.

Keeping all this in mind, Teresa needs to recall the many positive things that she has done to build a good relationship with Eduardo—and she needs to use some of those strategies to deal with the current situation. Reminding herself of these points will help her calm down, focus and maintain perspective.

© 2011 CAMH

RELATIONSHIP BOOSTERS

Respect your teen

Respect your teen and his feelings and opinions, even if you don't always agree with his ideas and the things he does.

Trust your teen

Your teen may make mistakes or poor decisions at times—you can help out in these situations if you believe that she is trying her best. Here are some tips:

- Instead of punishing or berating your teen for making a poor choice, help him figure out how to choose better next time. Talk through the available options.

- Show that your expectations have not changed. If your teen gets the message that you think she will make bad decisions and get out of control in the teen years, she probably will. Don't be influenced by that stereotype.

- Let your teen know that whatever the problem, he can come to you. Even if you are unhappy with your teen, you will always be there to help.

- Trust that your teen will learn from the mistakes she makes. Let her know that you believe in her.

Be ready to listen—anytime

Even if it's not convenient for you and the topic does not seem to be important, listen if your teen wants to talk—this doesn't happen often enough so, when it does, don't let the opportunity slip by (this usually

© 2011 CAMH

happens at about 2:00 a.m.). Your teen needs to believe that no matter what he gets into, you will listen and support him. Your teen should always feel that you will help, even if you are not happy with his behaviour.

Spend time with your teen

The stereotype that most teens don't like their parents is untrue. Many parents and teens argue, but most teens love their parents and enjoy spending time with them.

Be non-judgmental

Ask for and listen to your teen's ideas, opinions and explanations in a manner that conveys interest and respect. Let your teen know that you think what she has to say is important. It's okay to disagree and offer counter opinions, but make sure that you avoid any derogatory comments or put-downs.

Give your teen the benefit of the doubt (once he's shown responsibility)

Expect that your teen will do his best. If you've seen him make responsible decisions in the past, encourage more. On the other hand, if your teen has a history of behaving inappropriately and deceiving you, you will want to be cautious and then gradually lenient as he exhibits more responsible behaviour.

Don't make assumptions

Get information—such as where she is going, how she's getting there, who she'll be with and other relevant details.

© 2011 CAMH

Be respectful of your teen's friends

Your teen's friends are important to her. Be respectful of them, make them feel welcome in your home and make an effort to get to know them. (Note: Watch the boundaries here—you are a parent, not one of the friends.)

Support your teen in avoiding or leaving a "bad" situation

There are times when your teen may want you to help her get out of a difficult situation. For example, if your teen wants to get away from a group of friends she is having trouble with, help her do it. This could involve your teen using your rules as an excuse for why she can't do something with them, or it could mean helping her switch classes or schools.

Set priorities—don't argue with your teen about everything

There may be many things you would like your teen to do or not do. For example, around the house you may want him to keep his room clean, do his laundry, set the table, wash dishes, walk the dog, do his homework and maintain regular grooming habits. You may also encourage him to have a part-time job. You likely don't want him to play his music loudly, throw his school books on the floor when he comes into the house or leave plates of half-eaten food in his room. It is important to decide which of these things are most important to you and work with your teen to see that they are done, while letting go of some of the other things—otherwise you may find yourselves caught up in endless arguments.

Support your teen to build relationships with other caring adults

Create and support opportunities for your teen to develop relationships with other adults whom you trust and respect. This may happen through involving your teen in regular extended family gatherings or

© 2011 CAMH

encouraging her to participate in recreational, sports or social groups where she may develop positive relationships with adult coaches and mentors.

Get to know whose opinions your teen values—and whom he might take advice from

Teens benefit from having a network of caring people they can count on. If you can't talk to your teen, or if he won't talk to you, think about whom he might talk to (i.e., someone you and your teen trust, such as a cousin, friend or aunt). You could ask the identified person to have a discussion with your teen—hearing that people share your opinions and values reinforces your messages to your teen.

BALANCE SENSITIVITY AND FIRMNESS

Finding the balance between sensitivity and firmness is one of the biggest challenges parents face. It is essential that your teen knows what your expectations are and what your underlying values are. The "house rules" need to be clear; at the same time, you must be flexible and renegotiate the rules as your children mature.

You don't want to be overly permissive and accepting of risky, potentially dangerous behaviour, yet you need to be able to live with the fact that most teens experiment (keeping in mind that most teens become well-functioning, productive adults), and that they will violate your best advice and rules on many occasions.

In the situation we described earlier, Teresa needs to keep this in mind as she explores the situation with her 15-year-old son, Eduardo. She needs to decide which issues she wants to focus on: Marijuana use (she doesn't know for sure who used it)? Marijuana use in her home?

© 2011 CAMH

Eduardo having a friend over when she was out (she is not even sure who was there)? The mess in the basement? The loud music that might disturb the neighbours?

Teresa has a lot of things to sort through with Eduardo. It will be important for her to initiate a conversation that Eduardo can engage in, so that they can begin to address Teresa's concerns. Until they begin the conversation, Teresa doesn't know if Eduardo has concerns and what they are. Teresa will need to approach Eduardo in a sensitive manner as she starts to consider what actions to take, including whether rules need clarification or renegotiation and what supervision and supports Eduardo may need. She also needs to consider the impact on her 18-year-old daughter, Maria, and Maria's possible role in the situation that took place.

Consider all sides of a situation

Sometimes your teen's judgment may be better than your own, as she may be aware of different aspects of a situation. Consider the following scenario:

> In May's family, the rule is that all family members make it a
> priority to attend all extended family events. May is 14 and, for
> the first time, is refusing to attend her aunt's birthday celebra-
> tion. May's mother remembers that May always looked forward
> to going to these family events and, especially when she was
> younger, would talk for weeks before the event about the fun
> games she would play with her cousins. May's mother doesn't
> know that last Christmas when they were at their grandmother's
> for dinner, May noticed that her older cousins were laughing
> together about the times they had gotten drunk, and she saw
> them sneak some beers into one of the bedrooms. She also
> overheard the boys talking about girls in a way that made her
> feel uncomfortable.

© 2011 CAMH

There are no clear rules that suit all teens in all situations. It is important to be able to have an open, honest conversation so that your teen can feel heard, respected and supported, and so that both you and your teen can make good choices. In the scenario above, if May can discuss her experiences and concerns, and if her mother believes her and supports her, they could make a decision together as to whether or not May attends the family birthday celebration. If they agree that she attend, May and her mom can plan some strategies to keep May feeling safe and comfortable in a situation that is changing as the children are growing up. If May is not able to share her concerns with her mother, and her mother insists on sticking to "the rule" of attending family events, she may inadvertently put May in a risky situation.

The balancing act

Parents often find themselves facing complex decisions and, as discussed earlier, they look to find a balanced approach to difficult situations. There is "a fine line" between being too rigid and too lenient; between perceptions of "right" and "wrong."

Negotiate appropriate limits suited to your teen and the situation

When making decisions and establishing rules, it is often helpful to discuss with your teen what he sees as appropriate limits. Having input into establishing rules and limits helps teens feel respected, heard and trusted. Teens are more likely to follow rules that they were involved in making.

Have positive expectations and be realistic

Teens generally want to please their parents. Teens are more likely to meet their parents' expectations when they know their parents expect them to (not because they think their parents will punish them), when they understand the expectations and when the expectations make sense to them (especially if they were involved in creating them). So, having positive expectations is important—and it is important to be realistic.

© 2011 CAMH

Teens are growing and changing—and the rules and expectations that were appropriate one day may need revising or renegotiating the next.

Be flexible

Teens need parents to play roles that suit the situation. They may need you to play the decision maker to get them out of a bad situation (even if they don't appreciate it now, they will later). Other times they might need a friend to talk to, and it's okay to be that person too.

Negotiate consequences suited to your teen and the situation

Similar to negotiating rules and expectations, negotiating consequences (should the rules and expectations not be met) results in more meaning-ful consequences and perhaps greater likelihood that the rules will be followed. It is best to negotiate potential consequences prior to the rule not being followed. For example, before your teen leaves for a party, discuss what the consequences will be if she comes home later than planned.

EMPHASIZE SAFETY, RESPONSIBILITY AND OBEYING RULES

Keeping your children safe is of paramount importance. And, as already discussed, danger seems to lurk everywhere when you are a parent.

Perhaps when Teresa takes the time to think about why her initial response to the situation with Eduardo was anger, she may realize that she is afraid that the odour of marijuana in the house signals the begin-ning of a slippery slope to increasingly dangerous situations. She may think that she has failed in her role as a parent and hasn't provided Eduardo with the tools he needs to navigate the challenges of adolescence success-fully. However, if she can contain her feelings, she can work with Eduardo to reinstate appropriate rules and limits for him, and to determine what he needs from her to help him make good choices and stay safe. She could also seek social support for herself from friends who have similar values.

© 2011 CAMH

Recognize that some teens are more vulnerable than others

In addition to the stresses inherent in adolescence in our society, some teens may feel vulnerable and experience even more stress because of their gender, culture or race, sexual orientation, religion or spirituality, abilities, interests, or even the school they attend.

Here are some examples:

- Despite the movement away from gender stereotypes and roles, many people still have specific ideas about how boys and girls should think and behave—and these ideas about gender are reinforced by society, including parents, teachers, peers, communities and the media. Teens who don't fit the gender stereotype (such as girls who excel at math or boys who study ballet) may find other students isolate or tease them. Or their parents and other adults may not respect their choices and encourage them to follow paths that are more "normal" for their gender.

- Teens who realize they are gay may struggle with "coming out" or "playing it straight" to fit in. Their hesitancy to be who they are and want to be is understandable, because they have observed that being gay is so stigmatized in our society that one of the worst insults is to call someone gay, whether they are or not.

- Teens who are aboriginal or newcomers to Canada may find themselves in schools where they do not speak the language well and where the customs and belief systems differ from those they experience at home.

It is most important not to generalize about how these stressors might affect teens and to find out what each stressor means to each individual teen. The key is to ensure that your teen has the skills to make the best decisions for himself, given the information he has available, his particular situation and the resources available to him.

© 2011 CAMH

SAFETY BOOSTERS

Following are some suggestions to help keep your teen as safe as possible.

Be available and accessible

Your teen needs to know that she can call you anytime to pick her up. Create a signal whereby your teen can let you know that you are to call her and insist she come home. This allows your teen to get out of an uncomfortable situation with only the embarrassment of a call from her parent—a small price to pay instead of having to go into a risky situation. Maintain your teen's trust in you—if you tell her she can call you anytime, don't punish her for calling too late.

Pay attention to any changes in your teen's mood or behaviour

Let your teen know if you think he is unusually quiet, sad, exuberant or happy. Let him know that you care and are there for him to talk to about what is going on in his life. Explore what may account for a change in his mood or behaviour. If it is something positive, this will create the opportunity to share a joyful moment. If it is something troublesome, it may provide an opportunity for you to support your teen or assist him in getting help if he needs it.

Be aware of the stresses your teen faces

Know your teen—and what is likely to affect her. How, for example, does she approach new situations—is she more likely to be tentative or to take risks?

© 2011 CAMH

Help your teen develop skills to choose friends and peer groups who are more likely to make healthy choices

Spend time talking to your teen about how he likes to spend his time. For example, explore with him the kinds of friends he likes to spend time with and the kinds of things he likes to do with his friends.

Teach him to be assertive, rather than passive or aggressive, when making choices. Give him strategies and skills to say no to his friends if they plan to engage in activities he doesn't want to be part of: Delay ("maybe later"); refuse ("no, I do not want to do that"); negotiate ("I'll bring something to the party, but not alcohol").

Be supportive

Offer suggestions to help your teen focus on what needs to be done. For example, if she is stressed about schoolwork, don't berate her for doing badly on a test.

Help your teen develop problem-solving skills

Well-developed problem-solving skills will help your teen make good decisions in difficult situations. She needs to be able to identify what the problem is and what the options are before she can weigh the pros and cons and make the best decision. Teach her questions she can ask herself: Will this be good for me? Will I be happy with myself if I make this choice?

Provide your teen with reliable and practical information

Make sure your teen is informed of the dangers of certain situations (but don't be alarmist!) and knows what options are available. If he

© 2011 CAMH

has the facts, he is more likely to make informed decisions rather than impulsive ones. Practical information may include:

- who to call when he is in an uncomfortable situation—you, of course, and a couple of other trusted adults who are aware they could be called

- how to call and pay for a taxi, or if your teen has a smart phone, go to www.arrivealive.org to get a free application (app) that has Canada-wide taxi and transit-system information

- what to have on hand in case of an emergency (extra cash, but not too much)

- tips about safer ways to use alcohol and other drugs (just in case), such as:

  - pace yourself—it takes a while to feel the effects of alcohol

  - don't drink on an empty stomach

  - drink a lot of water

  - be with good friends who will take care of you

  - don't go by yourself, or with people you barely know, to a party where you don't know anyone else.

Provide supervision

- Know where your teen is, who she is with and what she is doing (as much as possible). Know what you have in your home—and think about the temptations and pressures created by what is in your home (e.g., alcohol, medication, Internet access).

© 2011 CAMH

TEACH—DON'T JUST CRITICIZE

We often think of teaching as giving advice. Yet we know that we often learn best from watching others, from our own experiences, from discussing issues and challenges with others and by looking at situations from different perspectives. Teachers whom we trust and, who trust and believe in us are most effective in conveying information. They can get us to try new things or to look at situations in a different way.

Develop a mutually respectful and trusting relationship with your teen

Teens learn best when they have a mutually respectful and trusting relationship with their parents or other caring adults. They are most open to learning when they feel they won't be judged and criticized, when they know their efforts will be rewarded, and when the information is useful and clear. Consistency between what you say and what you do is crucial. Modelling appropriate behaviour and choosing helpful messages will be discussed in more detail in the next chapter.

Consider Teresa's challenge: She needs to think about what she has taught Eduardo, what he knows and needs to be reminded of, and perhaps what new things he needs to learn. Teresa needs to find a moment to talk to Eduardo: She needs to consider what messages she has already given Eduardo about her expectations and her values; and she needs to work with him to sort out the challenges he faced that day, to look at the overall challenges he has been facing lately and to help him get the information he needs to make good choices for himself.

© 2011 CAMH

COMMUNICATION BOOSTERS

Here are some tips for building and maintaining good communication with your teen.

Be a good role model and be aware of the messages you send

Consider the impact of your behaviour on your teen. For example, how much time do you spend on the Internet, watching TV or isolating yourself from the family? What do you do on the Internet? Work? Socialize? Play games? Gamble? Do you smoke, drink, use illegal drugs, gamble or take medication to manage your moods? What do you spend money on? What kind of language does your teen hear you using?

Remember: Teens may not listen to everything you tell them—yet they generally hear everything you say and notice everything you do.

Be clear about your values related to risk-taking behaviours

Your teen often learns about your values by listening to you discuss other topics (e.g., things in the news, friends' children)—even if you are chatting with friends and think he may not be paying attention or think the topic is important. Be careful not to moralize or be too judgmental: If your teen finds himself in situations similar to the one you were discussing, he likely won't feel comfortable talking to you about it because he will assume that he knows what you are going to say.

Make no subject taboo

The more uncomfortable the topic, the more likely that it is important to discuss. It is essential that you listen to your teen and show

© 2011 CAMH

an interest in her life and respect her opinions. She will be more willing to talk to you if she thinks you are making an effort to understand her perspective and care about her opinion. Her opinions and ideas may not make sense to you. If you don't understand, ask her to explain.

Teach your teen conflict-resolution skills

By observing you as you resolve differences and by resolving differences with you, your teen learns how to deal with conflicts in his daily life. Here are some essential skills you can share with your teen:

- You don't always have to give in.
- You don't always have to win. Seek solutions where everyone can feel good about the outcome.
- Learn when to speak out and when to walk away.
- Do not compromise your values.

_____

© 2011 CAMH

Strategies for effective parenting: Messages to give your teen

As a parent, you need to think about the messages you give your teen. Sometimes you communicate messages directly—but much of the time you communicate messages indirectly. In other words, you often send your teen messages without planning to and without thinking about what messages you are communicating.

During adolescence, while teens strive to become more adult-like, it is especially important to pay attention to the messages you send out. Even though it may seem like your teen is not paying attention, she is observing you and trying to make sense of adult behaviour—and all the while learning from you.

Consider the following scenario and the messages Lise might be inadvertently sending her teenaged son, Claude.

Lise began to notice changes in Claude shortly after he started Grade 9. She had read about "the teenage years" and had started to dread them before they began. Now that they are here, she is anxious and worried that she and Claude will not make it through them. Lise finds it relatively easy to give Claude the space and privacy he needs—it's the demanding of independence and freedom that makes her nervous. "I know I can't keep him locked up in his room all night, but I also know what happens at those parties: It's the alcohol, other drugs and sexual relationships I am worried about. He can barely make himself breakfast. How can I trust that he knows how to handle the pressures about trying these things?"

© 2011 CAMH

If Lise shares her detailed concerns with Claude, what messages is she giving him and with what possible results?

Possible messages: Lise expects problems. She is fearful and worried for Claude, and for herself. She doesn't think Claude has the skills to take care of himself or to make good decisions, and she doubts her own ability to parent successfully through this time.

Possible results: Claude will expect problems—in fact, he may expect "big" problems since his mother suddenly seems unsure about things. Claude may feel it will be impossible to keep his mother happy and reduce her worry, especially while he tries to do "normal teenage things" such as having a bit more freedom and independence. Claude will think his mother doesn't have confidence in his abilities and this may lead him to doubt himself. As a result, he may not have the confidence he needs to make difficult choices.

Claude will not want to talk about his concerns or the challenges he faces with his mother out of fear that what he says will cause her more anxiety, and she may overreact. As a result, Lise will have fewer opportunities to teach and guide Claude about how to handle the pressures he is facing and the decisions he needs to make.

So what messages should you directly and indirectly be giving your teen? We've grouped the most important messages into the following categories:

- messages about your role as a parent
- messages about what you know and understand about the pressures teens face
- messages about the importance of safety
- messages about communication and your relationship with your teen.

© 2011 CAMH

We look at each of these messages below, especially in the context of teen smoking, drinking, use of other drugs, gambling and Internet use.

MESSAGE: "I STILL HAVE AN IMPORTANT ROLE TO PLAY IN YOUR LIFE"

Parents remain a primary influence in their children's lives throughout the teen years. You and your teen will benefit from understanding how important you continue to be to one another as your relationship evolves.

Be a role model

As a parent, you have a powerful influence over your teen's behaviour, especially those behaviours that have higher risks associated with them, like smoking, drinking, other drug use, gambling and some forms of Internet use. Your teen looks to you to learn about how to sort through problems and make decisions in all aspects of his life, including the more challenging ones.

To learn about these things, your teen may ask you direct questions— or she may simply watch how you deal with similar issues or problems. Take a look at what you say and do about these issues to ensure that you are sending messages that will help your teen make healthy choices.

Let's take a look at some messages you may send without intending to.

PARENTAL ACTIONS OR WORDS	MESSAGE TO TEEN
You celebrate every achievement or social occasion with alcohol.	Alcohol is for celebrating—drinking is something you can do to have fun.
"I've had a stressful day—I think I'll have a glass of wine."	Alcohol is for relaxing—and alcohol changes how you feel.
"I can't think yet—I haven't had my morning coffee."	Caffeine helps you think—and caffeine helps you function well.

© 2011 CAMH

PARENTAL ACTIONS OR WORDS	MESSAGE TO TEEN
"I wish we would win the lottery—then our lives would be better."	Gambling can lead to a better life.
You are amused or entertained by someone's drunken behaviour.	Being drunk is acceptable—and positive.
You have fun smoking marijuana with friends: "It's natural and safe." (Yes, we mean some parents say and do this.)	Smoking cannabis is acceptable—and positive.
You reminisce about the "good old days," including the parties and the times you don't remember how you got home.	Extreme intoxication is not risky—everything turns out okay.
You are critical of other parents or teens for their approaches to dealing with these types of issues.	Mom or dad will criticize me if I try to talk to them about these types of issues.

You are an important role model. The first thing you need to do is examine your actions and words—you may discover that you need to make changes to yourself in order to convincingly give your teen the messages you would like him to receive and follow. Think, for example, about some of the messages you may be giving your teen by your own substance use– or gambling–related words and actions. Ask yourself how your words and your actions fit with your hopes for and expectations of your teen.

Expect the best from your teen

As a parent you have tremendous power in creating expectations—both positive and negative—for your children. This does not change in adolescence: If you communicate to your teen that you think she cannot make good decisions, she may question her ability to make healthy choices. If you communicate that street drug use is rampant amongst teenagers and that teenagers rarely contribute to society in positive ways, your

© 2011 CAMH

teen may identify unhealthy peer behaviour as normal or okay rather than as problematic. If you communicate that you expect your relationship with your teen will be full of conflict and that she will not want to spend time with you, your teen may be reluctant to seek your company or your advice. Negative expectations are more likely to lead to the negative results you—and your teen—do not want.

Knowing the facts and communicating positive messages help achieve the outcomes you and your teen *do* want. Research shows that:

- Three out of four teens (75 per cent) report happy and pleasant relationships with their parents—and that the remaining 25 per cent of teens who were not so happy had histories of difficulties that preceded adolescence

- When there are differences of opinion between parents and teens, teens are far less likely to interpret these differences as significant to the relationship—and it is quite likely that conflict will decrease over time as parents and teens adjust to teens' increasing need for privacy and autonomy.

Keeping these facts in mind puts you in a better position to enjoy your teen throughout the teen years. It will also help your teen—and enhance your relationship with her.

Guide your teen by knowing the facts

It is important to know the facts about experimentation and the effects and potential dangers of the risk activities discussed in this book. Credibility is important to teens. Absolute or extreme statements by parents will likely be countered with "yes, but" answers that reflect opposing views—often the exact views parents don't want their teens to hold. Instead, effective parents engage teens in discussions that encourage them to consider the risks and benefits of new or ongoing activities. This helps teens think through things for themselves and gives them opportunities to talk about the possible negative consequences. This exercise is far more powerful

© 2011 CAMH

than telling your teen that you expect her to behave badly and that there will be negative consequences as a result.

As has been discussed earlier in this book, most teens will experiment with smoking, drinking alcohol, using other drugs and gambling at some time during adolescence. Attempting to ban this normal, curiosity-based behaviour will likely do little to reduce your teen's participation in these activities—and will likely do more to reduce his willingness to engage in discussions about these activities. Instead, exercise your continuing influence as a parent by:

- demonstrating concern
- giving clear messages about safety, choice and responsibility
- encouraging and motivating your teen to deal with issues that concern him through discussion and making healthy choices.

As your teen tries some of these new behaviours, she will likely discover there are positive aspects to them: She may experience reduced feelings of stress; improved mood and a perceived sense of "fun"; greater peer acceptance; and an enhanced sense of autonomy. Your teen will need encouragement and support from you to find other ways to achieve these appropriate goals (e.g., less stress, elevated mood) so that she can choose meaningful alternatives to these risky behaviours.

Continue to talk directly to your teen about smoking, drinking, using other drugs, gambling and Internet use as his needs and experiences change. You may be surprised to find that your teen is quite interested in talking to you about these risk behaviours because he may feel inundated with different messages from different sources and unsure about what is right for him. If you don't know the answers to the questions your teen asks, you can work together to find the answers. This will help him see you are trying to provide accurate information instead of giving responses based on inflexible rules. Through understanding your teen's experiences, perceptions and questions around risk behaviours and providing him with informed guidance, you can

© 2011 CAMH

maintain your influential role by helping to shape when, how and with what your teen experiments.

Monitor—and support—your teen's well-being

Your role as a parent gives you unique insights into your teen. When she was younger, you undoubtedly monitored her health; how she was feeling about things; and how she was doing at school, with friends and in the community. And you would have let her know how you expected her to behave.

This does not change when your child becomes a teenager. You'll want to continue to monitor his well-being and provide him with guidance in all areas of his life. The challenge with teens is that they will likely engage in some riskier behaviours, with consequences that can be potentially more serious than anything they've gotten themselves into before.

Effective parents take the time to explore what is going on with their teens across all aspects of their teens' lives—and they resist the temptation to focus exclusively on the risky behaviours. This sends the important message that, as a parent, you are interested in knowing about and understanding your teen's experiences and how these experiences affect her life—you're not just interested in the parts of her life that may be the source of some conflict between you.

Just as you did when your teen was younger, you'll want to explore changes in functioning with compassion, empathy and support. Sometimes changes in functioning and experimentation with risky behaviours (such as alcohol use) may occur around the same time in adolescence. This does not necessarily mean that the risky behaviour is causing the problem: Your teen may have chosen alcohol use as a way of coping with other difficulties in his life—and it is these difficulties that need to be addressed.

You know and understand your child better than anyone and should not ignore significant changes in how she performs in any areas of her life. Do not assume that the significant changes in how your teen performs are a normal part of adolescence. (See pages 24–28 for a description of the warning signs to watch out for.) If your teen starts to experience significant difficulties in any areas of his life, get help immediately for your teen and for the rest of the family. Your teen's main social sphere is the family—and it is within that context that his issues need to be explored.

MESSAGE: "I UNDERSTAND THE PRESSURES YOU FACE"

It is important for you, as a parent, to communicate the message that you are aware of and appreciate the pressures your teen faces—pressures to be successful and popular, as well as pressures to try new and risky behaviours (such as smoking, drinking, using other drugs and gambling). You can do this by offering your teen guidance, encouragement and support, and by showing a genuine interest in his life.

Ask your teen how you can help her cope with these pressures. Help her explore different strategies for dealing with these pressures—and try to reduce the pressures you put on her.

One key way to increase your teen's resources for coping with the pressures he faces is to accentuate the positive in your relationship with him. Find as many opportunities as possible to initiate positive conversations with your teen and to highlight his positive attributes.

As we've mentioned earlier, you'll want to balance sensitivity with firmness. You help your teen cope with pressures by having clear, realistic expectations (that are discussed and understood in advance) about risk-taking behaviours and clear consequences if she breaks rules and undermines your trust.

After ensuring that rules are appropriate and relevant, predictability and consistency are the most important features of effective limit-setting and consequences. Inflexible, inappropriate rules that do not sensitively reflect the pressures faced by teens are likely to increase conflict, as will unpredictable and inconsistent enforcement of rules.

© 2011 CAMH

Consider the following example:

Michael and his parents agreed that Michael was allowed to go to parties as long as he did not come home intoxicated, did not get into a vehicle with a driver who had been drinking or using other drugs, and arrived home by curfew. For two months Michael followed the first two rules consistently, and he mostly came home on time. A few times he had been up to an hour late, but his parents didn't say anything to him about it because they were happy that everything else in his life was going fine. Last night, Michael came home 35 minutes late—and his mother saw him passionately kissing a girl outside the house. Michael's mother overreacted to these events by telling Michael that he was always violating their trust by being late and by grounding him for a month. Michael, furious, replied: "There's obviously no point in following the rules—you don't trust me anyway."

What is going on between Michael and his parents? How could this situation have played out differently?

When Michael's parents did not speak to Michael about his lateness on previous occasions, they may have communicated to him that the rule about lateness was less important than the other rules. Michael may have interpreted this as meaning that his parents trusted him to use his judgment. Using Michael's late arrival home on previous occasions as reasons for her strong response to his current lateness (it's probably concern about his sexual behaviour that's really upsetting her), Michael's mother could confuse him (it was okay to come home late on other occasions but not on this occasion) about the importance of the rules and this could increase the likelihood of conflict between them in future.

© 2011 CAMH

Another way you can help your teen deal with pressures is by coaching him, either directly or indirectly, in social problem-solving skills. For example, you could talk openly and honestly about social pressures you experienced in different areas of your life—and explore with your teen how you felt in the particular situation, solutions you considered and why you considered them, solutions you felt you should use and why, and how you reached a decision and proceeded. Your teen learns important lessons from seeing and understanding how you deal with various pressures.

You can also teach strategies for dealing with difficult situations by role-playing with your teen, providing her with language to use and giving concrete, relevant examples.

MESSAGE: "I WANT YOU TO BE SAFE"

It is vital that you clearly communicate to your teen the importance of making safe choices. You can help by ensuring that your teen has as much information as possible to make safe, informed choices. While it may seem obvious to adults what level of risk is associated with each choice, it may not be as obvious to teens who have less experience; may be less likely to consider consequences; and are more likely to focus on other priorities such as independence, fitting in and having a good time. By emphasizing safety—rather than arbitrary rules and consequences—you maintain the familiar and important role you have had since your child was born.

With the possibility of more risk behaviours coming into your teen's life, you need to help him explore and understand the possible dangers of engaging in these behaviours—and don't assume he knows! The dangers can include:

- physical and mental health consequences from using substances (especially from frequent use, long-term use, bingeing and overdosing)
- being assaulted while intoxicated

© 2011 CAMH

- using poor judgment and engaging in impulsive and/or dangerous behaviours while intoxicated (such as driving, swimming, gambling or engaging in what your teen would otherwise consider to be unwanted sexual behaviour)
- legal consequences (such as having her driver's licence suspended for drinking and driving)
- school consequences (such as missed classes and falling grades)
- relationship consequences (such as conflicts with parents, friends and teachers)
- financial consequences (such as losing a job or repeatedly losing money gambling).

Delay, delay and delay

The longer adolescents delay trying alcohol or other drugs, the greater the likelihood they will avoid dangerous situations and, more importantly, the greater the likelihood they will avoid developing problems with substance use. Supportive and caring role models—such as parents, teachers and other adults in teens' lives—are key to helping adolescents delay substance use.

Safety tips

You can help your teen reduce the risks related to smoking, drinking, using other drugs, gambling and Internet use by following these tips:

- Ensure that your teen learns through your actions and words that his safety is of high importance to you.
- Help your teen develop good problem-solving and decision-making skills regarding potentially risky behaviours—discuss where experimentation stops and problematic use starts.
- Help your teen learn to evaluate situations from the perspective of her safety—ask her about her concerns and worries.

© 2011 CAMH

- Know your teen's friends and their parents (if possible). What are their attitudes and behaviours with regard to smoking, drinking, using other drugs, gambling and Internet use?

- Know where your teen is, whom he is with, and how he will be getting home. Are smoking, drinking, using other drugs and gambling part of the plan, or likely to arise unexpectedly? (You are more likely to receive honest answers from your teen if you have a positive, respectful relationship with him.)

- Have a reasonable curfew for your teen.

- Teach your teen some practical skills, such as what to do if she can't get in touch with you, how to take a cab, and what to do if she becomes intoxicated.

MESSAGE: "I WANT TO HAVE A GOOD RELATIONSHIP WITH YOU"

To remain important in your child's life as he moves into the teen years, you must be sensitive to how he is changing, the pressures he faces and how your roles with each other may change. The most effective type of communication is communication that goes both ways. This may mean, for example, that you communicate with your teen about important issues like risk behaviours at times that are convenient and relevant for him (and not necessarily for you) and that you listen to him as much as or more than he listens to you.

At times you may find it difficult to stay calm and open to your teen's perspectives—especially if you find out things about her that concern you. There may be other times when you will have to focus your attention on your long-term goals of an open and honest relationship with your teen in order to not react in the moment to provocative statements or attitudes she displays.

© 2011 CAMH

Build trust and respect with your teen

Trust and respect are fundamental features of healthy relationships. Fathers and mothers who take an appropriate interest in their teens' activities and whereabouts—and who provide appropriate rules and restrictions in the context of a positive, engaging overall relationship—help their teens develop a more firmly grounded and positive view of themselves in relation to others.

Respect—or disrespect—can be communicated in every interaction. For example, if your teen wants to tell you about something that happened and you do not have the time or interest to hear about it, your teen may question how much you respect and value his relationship with you. If you intrude on your teen's privacy, he may think you do not respect his personal space. On the other hand, if you seek your teen's opinions about issues that matter to him or you engage him in thoughtful discussion, he will likely feel that you appreciate, respect and value your relationship with him. If you care about what your teen thinks, he is more likely to care about what you think.

AVOID "TRUST DESTROYERS"

Avoiding the following examples of "trust destroyers" will help you maintain a good relationship with your teen. Focus on the positives and practise the "insteads"—your relationship with your teen will be better if you do.

Avoid: Accusations.

Instead: Express concern with statements such as "I am worried that...."

© 2011 CAMH

Avoid: Searching, snooping and eavesdropping.

Instead: Engage your teen in open, honest and direct dialogue.

Avoid: Overgeneralizations about your teen, such as statements starting with "you always" or "you never."

Instead: Stick to the specific issue at hand. Remember that all of us, including teens, make mistakes and also do things well.

Avoid: Assuming the worst.

Instead: Give your teen the benefit of the doubt. She is likely doing her best to find a way through the complex and demanding pressures of being a teen in today's society.

Avoid: Reminders of past mistakes: Nobody likes to be repeatedly reminded of past failings.

Instead: Help your teen learn from his mistakes. Send him out again with new knowledge and skills—and your encouragement and support.

Avoid: Mistrust when trust is warranted: Some parents experience intense anxiety about the pressures and situations their teen will face; this can interfere with their ability to put reasonable trust in their teen.

Instead: If you are having difficulty trusting your teen—even though she has not done anything that would cause you to mistrust her— seek the support of friends, family, a counsellor or health care provider who can help you.

© 2011 CAMH

Words of wisdom

Times have changed—yet many things remain constant. Consider the words of notable others on the topic of parents and children.

I've never understood why people consider youth a time of freedom and joy. It's probably because they have forgotten their own.

— Margaret Atwood

Children have never been very good at listening to their elders, but they have never failed to imitate them.

—James Baldwin

Kind words can be short and easy to speak, but their echoes are truly endless.

—Mother Teresa

A person who never made a mistake never tried anything new.

— Albert Einstein

Parents can only give good advice or put them on the right paths, but the final forming of a person's character lies in their own hands.

— Anne Frank

The central struggle of parenthood is to let our hopes for our children outweigh our fears.

— Ellen Goodman

It's not only children who grow. Parents do too. As much as we watch to see what our children do with their lives, they are watching us to see what we do with ours. I can't tell my children to reach for the sun. All I can do is reach for it, myself.

— Joyce Maynard

© 2011 CAMH

References

Centre for Addiction and Mental Health. (2004). *Youth & Drugs and Mental Health: A Resource for Professionals.* Toronto: Centre for Addiction and Mental Health.

Feldman, L., Harvey, B., Holowaty, P. & Shortt, L. (1999). Alcohol use beliefs and behaviors among high school students. *Journal of Adolescent Health, 24,* 48–58.

Johnston, L.D., O'Malley, P.M., Bachman, J.G. & Schulenberg, J.E. (2007). *Monitoring the Future: National results on adolescent drug use: Overview of key findings, 2006.* NIH Publication No. 07-6202. Bethesda, MD: National Institute on Drug Abuse.

Paglia-Boak, A., Mann, R.E., Adlaf, E.M., Beitchman, J.H., Wolfe, D. & Rehm, J. (2010). *The Mental Health and Well-Being of Ontario Students, 1991–2009: Detailed OSDUH Findings.* CAMH Research Document Series No. 29. Toronto: Centre for Addiction and Mental Health.

Paglia-Boak, A., Mann, R.E., Adlaf, E.M. & Rehm, J. (2009). *Drug Use Among Ontario Students: 1977–2009.* CAMH Research Document Series No. 27. Toronto: Centre for Addiction and Mental Health.

Pepler, D.J., Craig, W.M., Connolly, J. & Henderson, K. (2002). Bullying, sexual harassment, dating violence, and substance use among adolescents. In C. Wekerle & A. Wall (Eds.). *The Violence and Addiction Equation: Theoretical and clinical issues in substance abuse and relationship violence.* (pp. 153–168). New York: Brunner-Routledge.

Rose, A.J. & Rudolf, K.D. (2006). A review of sex differences in peer relationship processes: Potential trade-offs for the emotional and behavioral develpment of boys and girls. *Psychological Bulletin, 132,* 98–131.

Swahn, M.H., Bossarte, R.M. & Sullivent, E.E. (2008). Age of alcohol use initiation, suicidal behavior, and peer and dating violence victimization and perpetration among high-risk, seventh-grade adolescents. *Pediatrics, 121* (2), 297–305.

Wolfe, D.A. (2007). *What Parents Need to Know about Teens: Facts, Myths and Strategies.* Toronto: Centre for Addiction and Mental Health.

Wolfe, D.A., Jaffe, P. & Crooks, C.C. (2006). *Adolescent Risk Behaviors: Why Teens Experiment and Strategies to Keep Them Safe.* New Haven, CT: Yale University Press.

© 2011 CAMH

Resources for parents

If you are looking for more information on the topics we've discussed in this book, you may find the following resources useful.

BOOKS

Barkley, R.A. & Robin, A.L. (2008). *Your Defiant Teen: 10 Steps to Resolve Conflict and Rebuild Your Relationship*. Guilford Publications.

Bradley, M.J. (2002). *Yes, Your Teen is Crazy! Loving Your Kid Without Losing Your Mind*. Harbor Press Inc.

Feinstein, S. (2009). *Inside the Teenage Brain: Parenting a Work in Progress*. Rowman & Littlefield Education.

Wolf, A.E. (2002). *Get Out of My Life, but First Could You Drive Me and Cheryl to the Mall: A Parent's Guide to the New Teenager*. Farrar, Straus and Giroux.

WEBSITES

American Academy of Child & Adolescent Psychiatry
The Facts for Families section of this website offers concise information on issues that affect children, teens and their families.

www.aacap.org

GetGameSmart.com
This website offers information and tips for teens and their families about TV shows, video games and the Internet.

www.getgamesmart.com

© 2011 CAMH

Media Awareness Network

This website provides information for parents and teachers around media literacy for young people. Areas of focus include video games and the Internet.

www.media-awareness.ca

Parent Action on Drugs

Parent Action on Drugs addresses issues of substance use in youth. It provides information for parents, youth, educators, health promoters and communities to create environments that help youth make informed choices.

www.parentactionondrugs.org

ProblemGambling.ca

This CAMH website provides a variety of resources, including information about gambling, problem gambling, how to get help and information for families.

www.problemgambling.ca

© 2011 CAMH

About the authors

David A. Wolfe is a clinical psychologist who has worked with children and teens for more than 30 years. He holds the RBC Chair in Children's Mental Health at the Centre for Addiction and Mental Health (CAMH), and is a professor of psychology and psychiatry at the University of Toronto. David lives in London, where he heads the CAMH Centre for Prevention Science that develops curricula for promoting healthy relationships among youth.

Debbie Chiodo is a researcher and centre manager at the CAMH Centre for Prevention Science in London. She oversees regional and provincial projects aimed at improving engagement and academic outcomes for youth. She has been part of the implementation and evaluation of school-based programming for youth in schools across Canada. She is committed to improving access and delivery of services to youth and supports the use of schools and community groups as pivotal entry points for the delivery of facilitation and support.

Bruce Ballon is a psychiatrist and an assistant professor in the University of Toronto's Faculty of Medicine. He is the director of the Psychiatry Simulation Innovation (PSI) Centre for the University of Toronto based at Mount Sinai Hospital. Bruce is the associate director for Education Scholarship in Simulation at the Network of Excellence in Simulation for Clinical Teaching and Learning (NESCTL) that encompasses the academic health centres in Ontario. He is also the head and developer of the new initiative Adolescent Clinical and Educational Services (ACES) for problem gambling, gaming and Internet addiction at CAMH.

Gloria Chaim is a social worker who has worked for more than 25 years with youth and families who have concerns related to addiction and mental health issues. She is the deputy clinical director in the Child, Youth and Family Program at CAMH. Gloria is committed to numerous projects related to prevention, early identification and increasing access to appropriate services for young people and their families.

Joanna L. Henderson is a clinical psychologist who has worked with children, youth and families for 15 years. She holds the position of independent clinician scientist with the Child, Youth and Family Program at CAMH. Her work focuses on understanding and addressing the needs of youth with substance use–and mental health–related concerns.

© 2011 CAMH

Acknowledgments

The authors would like to acknowledge everyone who reviewed an earlier draft of this book and gave us valuable feedback and suggestions for improvement.

Many thanks to the parent reviewers who gave us feedback based on their experiences parenting teens:

Kerry P. Clemen
Jasper Miller
Joan Vertes
Joëlle Viau
O. Thomas Weihmayr
Joy Wilcox
Bari Zittell.

Thank you to the health care professionals and educators—many of whom are currently parenting or have parented teens—who provided feedback:

Jane Fjeld, associate executive director, Youth Services Bureau of Ottawa

David Goldbloom, MD, FRCPC, senior medical adviser, Education and Public Affairs, CAMH; professor of psychiatry, University of Toronto; Vice-Chair, Mental Health Commission of Canada

Colleen Kelly, MSW, RSW, discipline chief, Social Work, CAMH

Christine Lebert, manager, Provincial Services, CAMH

Colleen McKinnon, teacher, Monetville Public School, Rainbow District School Board

Cynthia Osborne, MD, West London Family Health Clinic

Maureen Reid, MSW, RSW, program manager, Children's Aid Society, London, Ontario

Joanne Shenfeld, MSW, RSW, manager, Youth Addiction and Concurrent Disorders Service, Child, Youth and Family Program, Family Addiction Service, Addiction Program, CAMH

© 2011 CAMH

Lightning Source UK Ltd.
Milton Keynes UK
UKOW06f0037121117
312516UK00011B/646/P